LANDSCAPES FOR SMALL SPACES

LANDSCAPES
FOR SMALL SPACES
JAPANESE COURTYARD GARDENS

Photographs and text by
KATSUHIKO MIZUNO

Translated by **John Bester**

KODANSHA INTERNATIONAL
Tokyo · New York · London

TITLE PAGE: Mikami Residence

Note: The photographs in this book are printed with Diamond Screening, a technology that enables the reproduction of color artwork and photography which far surpasses the quality achievable by traditional printing methods.

Distributed in the United States by Kodansha America, Inc., 575 Lexington Avenue, New York N.Y. 10022, and in the United Kingdom and continental Europe by Kodansha Europe Ltd., 95 Aldwych, London WC2B 4JF. Published by Kodansha International Ltd., 17-14 Otowa 1-chome, Bunkyo-ku, Tokyo 112-8652, and Kodansha America, Inc.

CONTENTS

INTRODUCTION: The Tsuboniwa of Kyoto   vii

Palaces, Shrines, and Temples ——————— — ———— 1

Fujitsubo, Kyoto Imperial Palace   1

Hagitsubo, Kyoto Imperial Palace   4

Kamigamo Shrine   6

Matsunoshita-ya, Fushimi Inari Shrine   7

Kyokusui Garden, Matsunoo Shrine   8

Ninnaji Temple   10

Zuishin'in Temple   11

Rokudo Garden, Nanzenji Temple   12

Nanyoin Temple   14

Koshoji Temple   15

Tokaian Temple   16

Torin'in Temple   17

Daisen'in Temple   18

Kanmin Garden, Zuihoin Temple   19

Saiho Nunnery   20

Hokongoin Temple   21

Kanchiin
(a subsidiary temple of the Kyoo Gokokuji)   22

Sorenji Temple   23

Shojokein Temple   24

Totekiko Garden, Ryogen'in Temple   26

Kodaiji Temple   28

Taikoan Temple   29

Reikanji Temple   30

Daishin'in Temple   31

Honen'in Temple   32

Dongein Temple   34

Hokyoji Temple   35

Myorenji Temple   36

Shozenji Temple   37

Sanzen'in Temple   38

Chiekoin Temple   39

Ryojuin Temple   40

Genkoan Temple   41

Jurinji Temple   42

Murin'an   43

Townhouses 45

Ban Residence 46

Torii Residence 50

Ueno Residence 51

Kubo Residence (Hyoki) 52

Okamura Residence 53

Fujii Residence 54

Hata Residence 55

Nose Residence 56

Bokkai Residence 60

Yoshida Residence 61

Inoue Residence 62

Mikami Residence 64

Nakakura Residence 65

Matsumura Residence 66

Tatsumi Residence 68

Nishimura Residence 72

Ukai Residence 73

Private Residence 74

Gen'an 76

Public Places 81

Noguchi Residence (Karakuan) 82

Miyazaki Residence 86

Tanaka-ya 87

Rakusho 88

Shoeido 89

Nakazato 90

Tawara-ya 92

Kinmata 96

Tsuruya Yoshinobu 98

Hashimoto Teru Orimono 100

Shosuikaku, Nishijin Asagi 101

Orinasu Museum 102

Yamanaka Oil 103

Gekkeikan 104

Wada Residence 106

Machiya Photo Museum 107

Kahitsukan, Kyoto Museum of Contemporary Art 108

Kasuien, Westin Miyako Kyoto 110

APPENDICES 113

   Creating a Tsuboniwa—The Gen'an Garden 113
   Types of Stone Lantern 117

INDEX 119

The Tsuboniwa of Kyoto

Over its long history the Japanese garden has evolved into a variety of forms. One of these is known as *tsuboniwa*, which signifies a garden enclosed by different parts of a single structure such as a house or temple, forming a relatively small space cut off from the outside world. The original meaning of *tsuboniwa* is not entirely clear. Nowadays the word is usually written with the Chinese characters read *tsubo* (a unit of spatial measurement, approximately 3.3 meters square) and *niwa* (garden), though formerly *tsubo* was written with a different character also read *tsubo* and meaning "pot." This book is devoted to the tsuboniwa of Kyoto, where the finest examples of the genre are to be found.

The tsuboniwa has a long history. First recorded in the imperial palace in Kyoto during the Heian period, it formed an element of the residences of members of the warrior class during the following Kamakura period, then in Muromachi times was featured chiefly in temples of the Zen sect of Buddhism. Finally, in the Momoyama and early Edo periods, it became firmly established, and evolved into a definitive form as an essential part of the *machiya*, the characteristic townhouse of the merchant class.

The tsuboniwa has undergone many changes during its long history, preserving a variety of styles each related to the prevailing architectural style of the age. The buildings of the imperial palace during the Nara period (710–794), which stood separately, as independent structures, provided no enclosed space for such gardens, but the Heian period (794–1185) evolved a style of architecture, *shinden-zukuri*, in which a central building (the *shinden*) was flanked to right and left and to the rear by subsidiary structures, to which it was linked by open corridors. These buildings and corridors naturally created enclosed spaces.

The *Tsurezure-gusa* (Essays in Idleness), a collection of prose written by the Buddhist priest Yoshida Kenko toward the end of the Kamakura period (1185–1333), gives some advice concerning residential architecture. "Since Kyoto summers are intolerably hot," he says, "dwellings should be designed chiefly with summer in mind." In fact, astonishingly well-ventilated and comfortable dwellings had already been devised in the Heian period. The *shinden-zukuri* just mentioned employed a technique, depending basically on a framework of vertical and horizontal timbers, that made supporting walls and the like essentially unnecessary, and when independent buildings created in this way were linked by open corridors there were plenty of spaces for inner gardens—and plenty of points within the buildings whence they could be appreciated. A good example of such a garden is the Ryusentei of the Kyoto Imperial Palace, which lies on the way between two of its structures, the Osuzumi-dokoro and the Chosetsu.

The *Pillow Book* of Sei Shonagon relates that the tsuboniwa of the northern wing of the Seiryoden, residence of the empress Teishi, contained trees and other plants. In the *Tale of Genji*, names of court ladies, such as Kiritsubo ("Paulownia Garden") and Fujitsubo ("Wisteria Garden"), eloquently suggest the elegant lives they led in residences that looked out on private spaces planted with attractive trees and plants. In the existing Kyoto Imperial Palace, there are gardens called Fujitsubo and Hagitsubo (see pages 1–5) that give some idea of the size of tsuboniwa at that time.

With the beginning of rule by the warrior class, the emphasis in Japanese architecture shifted to what is known as the *shoin-zukuri* style. Shoin buildings, too, had their tsuboniwa. According to chronicles of the times, there were tsuboniwa—known, respectively, as Yomogi no Tsubo ("Mugwort Garden") and Ishi-tsubo ("Rock Garden")—in the residences of both Taira no Kiyomori and Minamoto no Yoritomo, leaders in the struggle between two powerful clans that led eventually to the establishment of the Kamakura shogunate under Yoritomo. These were smaller in area than those of the court. During the Kamakura period (1185–1333), the latter were sometimes used as places for unofficial interviews with persons of low rank who were not normally allowed into the court proper. However, despite differences in size, tsuboniwa, in imperial palace and samurai residence alike, developed in a sense as private spaces vital to the personal lives of the individuals concerned; in this respect they were quite different from the extensive gardens with ponds and running water that formed the "public" spaces fronting palace and mansion.

With the Muromachi period (1333–1573), the *shoin-zukuri* style of architecture was inherited by the temples of the Zen sect, and the tsuboniwa came to be designed, chiefly in the form of a "dry landscape" (*kare-sansui*) garden, as a spatial embodiment of enlightenment, the highest spiritual attainment of Zen. Two examples of such gardens, both officially designated as *meisho*, a title given to spots of outstanding scenic beauty, are those of the Shoin of the Daisen'in temple, and the Reiun'in temple.

Following its devastation in the Onin war (1467–77), the city of Kyoto was rebuilt, this time in better-planned form, by Toyotomi Hideyoshi. The homes of the merchant class were progressively reordered into blocks of dwellings, each of a well-defined long, rectangular shape, sharing the same roof. The unique type of townhouse that emerged presented a narrow front to the street but extended quite far from front to back. Popularly known as an "eel's lair," it made it possible to increase the area occupied by dwellings, and provided a highly efficient type of urban house combining workplace or place of business and residence. The shop, or space for doing business, which faced the main thoroughfare, was followed to the rear by the residential section, and behind that again by the production or storage area (though this area, as we shall see, later came to have other uses too). Thanks to this, work and business became more efficient. Taxes, which were decided according to the width of the facade, were kept down, and the development of commerce and industry was further promoted. As a result, the economic clout of the Kyoto merchants increased by leaps and bounds. Some idea of their past prosperity can be gained from the present splendor of the Gion festival, which was organized throughout the years by that increasingly affluent class.

With houses of a narrow rectangular shape adjoining each other beneath a single roof, light and ventilation, sufficient at the front of the house, deteriorated progressively toward the rear. To deal with this problem, an architectural style known as *omoteya-zukuri* was devised. In this *omoteya* style, the shop, or business wing, facing the main thoroughfare, was more or less independent, linked to the residential and reception wing (*omoya*) at its rear by an "entrance" wing.

Behind these in turn lay either—depending on the nature of the business—a storehouse to hold the goods in which the family dealt, or a place of work, or possibly a tea room or *hanare-zashiki* (separate quarters for other family members; see illustration below and photograph on page 45). The two spaces available for gardens between the sections served to let in light, provide ventilation, and keep the air moving. This arrangement served the double purpose of keeping the house cool in summer and providing the aesthetic comforts of a garden.

Well-established by the early Edo period (1603–1867), this relatively extravagant *omoteya* style of urban architecture was to continue as the predominant style of merchant home in Kyoto until the Taisho era (1912–26). The illustration below shows the house of a trader in raw silk situated in the Itoya Hatcho ("Eight Blocks of Silk Dealers") district of an area bordering on Omiya Street in Kamigyo ward. The residential (*omoya*) wing was put up in 1886 and the shop wing in the late Edo period, earlier in the same century, while one of the two storehouses is conjectured to have been built still earlier.

In the Itoya Hatcho district, incidentally, the owners were officially required to construct a two-story storehouse (storehouses were made to be more or less fireproof) at the rear of the site as a means of preventing fire spreading from a possible conflagration among the houses at the rear, from which it was separated only by a relatively narrow thoroughfare. In 1730, at the time of the Nishjin Fire that consumed 134 blocks in the Kamigyo area, the Itoya-machi district on Omiya Street did, in fact, escape involvement. A further advantage of these storehouses was that

OMOTEYA-ZUKURI *(the omoteya style)*

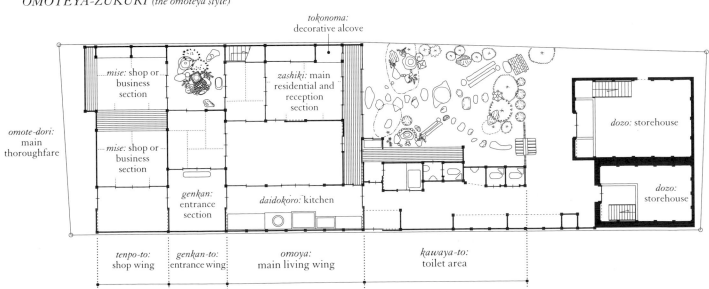

tokonoma: decorative alcove

mise: shop or business section

zashiki: main residential and reception section

omote-dori: main thoroughfare

mise: shop or business section

genkan: entrance section

daidokoro: kitchen

dozo: storehouse

dozo: storehouse

tenpo-to: shop wing

genkan-to: entrance wing

omoya: main living wing

kawaya-to: toilet area

the white plaster covering their outer walls reflected sunlight, benefiting the tsuboniwa and bringing extra light to the interior of the *zashiki* on the other side of the garden.

From Momoyama (1573–1603) on into the early Edo period (seventeenth century), a rigid class system deterred the merchants from indulging in costly custom-made gardens in the inner spaces of their townhouses, but as the development of commerce gave their livelihood increasing stability, they came to look on these spaces as a source of spiritual refreshment and an expression of personal taste. At the same time, the tea ceremony, in the definitive form given it by Sen no Rikyu in the Momoyama period, spread beyond the court and the high-ranking warrior class to the moderately affluent members of the merchant class. The small garden outside the tea room, which originally served simply to bring in light, gradually developed in both design and function until it became the *roji*, a short pathway-cum-garden that served as an aesthetically pleasing invitation to, and spiritual preparation for, the tea room proper. Ideally, its arrangement included, as atmosphere-definers, rustic-looking stepping stones, a low-set water basin (*tsukubai*) of simple, unpretentious appearance, and a stone lantern, preferably with an interesting pedigree.

However, frequent sumptuary edicts issued by the ruling Tokugawa shogunate forbade the spending of large sums on gardens, and it seems likely that a majority of the tsuboniwa of the merchant class were quite modest affairs. However, in the Great Tenmei Fire of 1788 and again in the Kinmon Incident of 1864 much of Kyoto was reduced to ashes. The city was rebuilt on both occasions, and the techniques of *machiya* architecture became increasingly refined. In the stable Taisho era that followed the turbulent years of the Meiji era, the techniques of architecture and garden design as seen in the *machiya* and tsuboniwa of Kyoto reached an unprecedented level of sophistication.

The tsuboniwa of Kyoto's traditional merchant-class dwellings as seen today owe their beauty to techniques bequeathed by successive generations of garden designers since the Heian period, and to their constant willingness to learn from the aesthetic sensibilities of each new age. Since the garden is created within the building itself, the beauty of craftsmanship of the parts of the building in contact with it—pentroofs and eaves; shoji and windows; walls, wainscots, and pillars; open verandas and corridors—interact in a complex fashion with constituents of the garden such as the *kutsunugi-ishi* ("footwear-removing stone"), stepping stones, washbasin, stone lanterns, and the carefully tended plants of the garden itself to create an exquisite universe in miniature.

Today, with the general loss of greenery, the trapping of heat in cities, and global warming, the time has perhaps come for a second look at an urban life dependent on the supposed benefits of modern civilization. At such a time as this, one looks with a fresh eye at the resourceful men of the past who designed urban dwellings with prime consideration for conditions in summer, together with their *omoteya* style of architecture. As they saw it, a dwelling should have two pocket gardens, one at the front and one at the rear. Thus in summer, if one splashes water on the tsuboniwa in the dimly lit entrance hall, the temperature there drops. The air, growing weightier as it cools, flows out toward the tsuboniwa at the rear of the residential and reception (*zashiki*) section. Here, there is light, and the air is less heavy. A current is thus set up that brings a cool breeze into the *zashiki*, functioning as a natural cooling system that may well be one factor that has helped keep the Kyoto *machiya* going for more than three centuries.

Generally speaking, the tsuboniwa in the entrance of a townhouse is two or three *tsubo* in area, and, like a *roji* (tea garden), has a water basin or a single stone lantern. As a garden it is small, surrounded by other parts of the house, with no direct sunlight and a bare minimum of low-lying vegetation, so that it impresses with a short-hand style of beauty similar to that of the "dry landscape" (*kare-sansui*) of the Zen temple. Situated as it is, it is open to the gaze of any visitor to the house.

The other tsuboniwa lies behind the *zashiki* section of the house, between that area and the *hanare-zashiki* or storehouse. Relatively spacious, with a variety of plants, it gets plenty of sunlight and shows the personal taste of the master of the house in various carefully calculated effects and touches of design such as a washbasin placed by the veranda and one, two, or even more stone lanterns of varied size. This garden at the rear is a private affair seen only by members of the family or acquaintances who are admitted to the living and reception wing. In most cases, it is surrounded by a veranda, and the washplace, bath, and toilet are close at hand. The two gardens represent, respectively, the everyday, public side of the family's life and the special, private side—a distinction aptly demonstrating the ingenuity and flexibility with which the people of Kyoto traditionally regulated their lives.

With the influx of Western-style rationalism since the end of World War II and the energy revolution involving the use of electricity and oil, the traditional *machiya* has given way to a new, more enclosed type of house. In order to make better use of scarce land and minimize the dangers of fire, it has been replaced in many cases by high-rise modern buildings. In today's Kyoto, it has become extremely difficult to maintain the old merchant dwellings with their beautiful tsuboniwa. Now everything is up to the efforts of a few, special individuals.

Yet, one still recalls the damp air scented with the fragrance of mosses wafted in from the tsuboniwa; the rain and the wind; the dusting of snow and the bright shafts of sunlight.... Times of spiritual refreshment, spent indoors and in the midst of the dense, crowded living spaces of the town, yet in constant companionship with the poetry of natural phenomena.... Surely, one feels, the tsuboniwa is precisely the kind of space that is essential to a healthy emotional and physical life.

Recently, people have been experimenting with the idea of tsuboniwa created for their visual effect in new, Western-style buildings or on rooftops, for which soil is specially transported, trees are planted, and rocks arranged. Others, it seems, have been doing research on types of moss that will grow on the walls of buildings or patches of bare earth where there is little moisture. In an artificial urban environment, people are beginning to seek out new ways of contacting nature and re-establishing types of space that are both relaxing and in tune with the age.

One can only hope that a new type of tsuboniwa will emerge, even while we continue to cherish the culture of the past.

Palaces, Shrines, and Temples

Many courtyard gardens created between the Heian and Tokugawa periods have survived to the present day, their beauty enhanced by the hands of time and the elements—small, pure worlds lying in a hushed grace in the remoter recesses of an imperial palace, or more stiffly correct and solemn in a Shinto shrine or Buddhist temple.

Fujitsubo, Kyoto Imperial Palace

The courtyard garden of the Higyosha, a building in a distant part of the palace. A single, eminently dignified wisteria vine grows on a stretch of silver sand surrounded by the elegant structures of the palace. One can still see here a prototype of today's tsuboniwa.

Hagitsubo, Kyoto Imperial Palace

An unpretentious garden situated at the rear of
the Seiryoden, the Emperor's personal quarters. Simplicity itself, the garden consists only
of twenty bushclover (*hagi*) plants; yet, surrounded as it is by buildings in the ancient
shinden-zukuri style, it breathes a courtly ele-
gance that marks it definitively as a tsuboniwa
of the Heian period.

Kamigamo Shrine

A five-meter-square space lying between a large room and an open connecting corridor, the garden consists of an expanse of fine white sand with a circular clump of bamboo planted at its center. In its straightforward simplicity it has a quiet dignity that perfectly matches the sacred atmosphere of an ancient Shinto shrine.

Matsunoshita-ya, Fushimi Inari Shrine

Lavish use is made of various types of unusual stone found in the Kyoto area. The water basin is set low, and the vegetation is correspondingly restricted to low shrubs, creating a simple, well-balanced composition. A satisfying contrast with this traditional tea garden is created by the modern design of the corridor railing and the white of shoji and plaster wall.

Kyokusui Garden, Matsunoo Shrine

The shrine offices are connected to two buildings, used for ceremonial purposes and to house the shrine's treasures, by a long, open corridor. The generous space thus formed is occupied by a garden with a stream that meanders gently between the rocks, its clear water provided by the Mitarashi River that runs down from the hills behind the shrine. The gentlenesss of the stream and the strength of the arrangement of high and low rocks on the azalea-planted hillock create a pleasing harmony.

Kyokusui Garden, Matsunoo Shrine

The azaleas on the hill, which are pruned rigorously in order to preserve the garden's original appearance, normally have a sparse showing of blooms, but once every five or six years they are covered with a mass of blossom that seems to fill the whole garden with crimson. One wonders if the designer of the garden had such an effect in mind.

Ninnaji Temple

A small garden enclosed by the open corridor leading from the Kuro-shoin to the Shinden. A small species of bamboo flourishes on a carpet of moss set with four smallish rocks. A sophisticated, tasteful garden that preserves the atmosphere of the traditional palace tsuboniwa.

Zuishin'in Temple

This garden was designed to be viewed from various angles. The rocks that give variety to the even carpet of moss blend well with the abundance of vegetation. In late spring and early summer, the most eye-catching features are the comparatively plain rhododendron, followed by the more colorful azalea.

Rokudo Garden, Nanzenji Temple

A long gallery leading from the Hojo to the Shoin makes a number of right-angle turns in its course, thus creating space for several tsuboniwa. The main one, known as the Rokudo Garden, is composed of three rocks symbolizing a triad of Buddhist divinities, together with several other ornamental rocks, set in an overall surface of moss against the background provided by a fence of thick woven bamboo. In autumn and summer respectively, the vegetation provides colorful touches in the form of crimson maple leaves and the refreshing pale pink blossom of crape myrtle.

Rokudo Garden, Nanzenji Temple

The Rokudo Garden seen on a snowy day. An unusual touch is added by a pillar stone called Bochuseki ("pillar-viewing rock") brought over from the Korean peninsula in ancient times.

Nanyoin Temple

An inner garden with a central Kasuga stone lantern and stepping stones, the main element in the composition being evergreens surrounding a well-shaped red pine. The arrangement may seem rather commonplace, but early in the year when the red damson blooms, the garden has a gay, springlike atmosphere. The tallish, beautifully shaped wash basin, which was originally a base-stone for the pier of a bridge, serves to pull the total effect together.

Koshoji Temple

This wash basin has long been well known as the "stepping-down" basin. Situated in the inner garden of the Kuri and surrounded by an oak hedge, it stands at the bottom of a hollow, so that to use it one has to descend a flight of steps. When one goes to wash one's hands, the feeling is of entering a somehow different world.

Torin'in Temple

A narrow, horizontally extended garden, barely two meters deep, lying between the Kyakuden and the Kuri. The bamboo fence, while ensuring the privacy of the latter, avoids any overbearing impression. The design of the garden, with its azaleas planted low at two different levels, has a surprisingly bold, modern feeling. The water basin shaped like a flattened metal bowl that stands in the center is a masterly touch.

◄ Tokaian Temple

An inner garden lying between the Hojo and the Shoin and entirely encircled by corridors. The whole space is covered with fine white sand, with seven small rocks arranged in a more or less straight line. This type of "dry landscape" effect, using mainly sand and rocks, with neither pond nor any other water, is used symbolically, with its intimations of a vast universe, to express the Zen spirit.

Daisen'in Temple

Lying between the Hojo and the Shoin, this tsuboniwa is known as Chukai ("inner sea"). The simple, cleancut arrangement of a few rocks and a well-house, together with a single camellia bush, has an unpretentious beauty. The Daisen'in also has another, far more imposing main garden, but the skill that created this utterly simple "dry landscape" garden ranks it unashamedly beside its more celebrated counterpart.

Kanmin Garden, Zuihoin Temple

The designer of this garden intended it as the north garden of the Hojo rather than as a tsuboniwa, but since its location—between those quarters and a tea room—is typical of a tsuboniwa, it can be introduced here as an outstanding example of the latter. The seven rocks arranged on a bed of white sand are said to form the shape of a cross, since the original founder of the temple, Otomo Sorin, was a Christian daimyo. The two different types of bamboo fence that mark off the garden are in no way intrusive, and help to integrate the whole.

Saiho Nunnery

This was intended as the outer roji of a tea room, but it can also be seen as a tsubo-niwa whose main attraction is the multicolored camellia said to have been planted personally by the celebrated tea master Sen no Rikyu. Whether compared with the bamboo fence in the background or the stone lantern standing near it, the great size of the azalea is commensurate with an age of four centuries or so. Here, the multicolored petals lie scattered beneath a late spring sun.

Hokongoin Temple

The inner garden of the temple is planted with a large number of hydrangeas. The quiet grace of their flowers, looming pale blue through the steadily falling rains of the monsoon season, somehow call to mind the courtly culture of the age of the Empress Taikenmon'in.

Kanchiin (a subsidiary temple of the Kyoo Gokokuji)

This "dry landscape" garden, designed to be viewed from any angle, is given abundant vitality by the low shrubs and the moss covering it. The "river" of white sand flowing beneath the connecting corridor winds on its way to pour into the "sea" of the main garden of the temple's Kyakuden (a National Treasure). The mastery of the garden's designer is apparent in the beauty of the rock groupings.

Sorenji Temple

This small temple located in Kitayama on the northern outskirts of Kyoto, a district celebrated as a source of Kitayama cedar with its long, branch-free trunks, possesses a small garden of an astonishing refinement for a country temple. A rectangular space marked off by flat granite stones has an arrangement of a few rocks set in a bed of smooth pebbles. It often snows in the area, and one is tempted to think that the designer of the garden made conscious use of flat rocks so that the snow, drifting in through a narrow opening, should settle on them.

Shojokein Temple

This garden, surrounded as it is by buildings such as the Hojo and a tea house, is designed to be viewed from any angle. As befits a temple garden, the rocks on top of the moss-covered hillock are said to represent Buddhist divinities. In early summer, the long hedge of azalea is covered with crimson flowers, as though making an offering to the buddhas.

Totekiko Garden, Ryogen'in Temple

When snow settles on one of these tiny gardens, symbolically embracing all the varied natural phenomena of the universe, it seems to intensify still further their symbolic and spiritual qualities. The utter simplicity of this particular tsuboniwa exerts a purifying influence on the minds of temple visitors.

Totekiko Garden, Ryogen'in Temple

A veritable "small jewel" of a garden created at the heart of the temple. As the ripples from a single drop of water extend into a mighty ocean, so a tiny tsuboniwa can symbolize the whole universe. Here, the rays of the sun that strike down into the garden add an important element to the composition. ▶

Kodaiji Temple

This garden is designed both to give pleasure to the eyes of visitors as they walk toward the Kyakuden, and to serve as a front garden for those quarters themselves. The rocks set in the moss against the background provided by a roofed, white plaster wall are intended to suggest a triad of Buddhist divinities. The wash basin, stepping stones, and the like are all rather massive, contributing to the leisurely feeling of the whole.

Taikoan Temple

A mighty universe suggested within a bare 3.3 square meters of space—a garden surrounded on all sides by an extremely elegant unroofed veranda made of bamboo combined in a swastika-pattern. The exquisiteness of the design is enhanced by the stone wash basin situated on white sand. The sense of tautness of design filling the garden is mitigated here by a single red camellia bloom placed in the wash basin.

Reikanji Temple

This garden, enclosed by temple buildings and an open gallery, is so full of maples
and azaleas that no rocks or the like are visible at all. So be it: this is the place famed
in Kyoto as the "flower temple," and one comes to enjoy, not so much the garden
proper, as the flowers of the various seasons that grow there. The azalea in particular makes a brilliant showing.

Daishin'in Temple

A garden bounded by the open corridor linking the Hojo, the Kuri, and the Shoin. The most striking feature is the huge, 360-year-old azalea, whose beauty when it blooms in early summer is enough to take the visitor's breath away.

Honen'in Temple

Between the main hall and the corridor fronting the Shoin, the Honen'in has an inner garden in which grow the three ancient, double-bloom camellia bushes that have given it the nickname "the camellia temple." Symbols of the temple, they serve both as floral offerings to the figure of Amida that is its main object of worship, and to delight the eyes of visitors passing along the corridor.

Dongein Temple

Situated between the temple's main hall and the Shoin, the whole garden is covered with two different types of moss. In the center, various kinds of rocks form an "island" on which grows a large camellia that was presumably intended originally either to afford a screen against the late afternoon sun or to give privacy against intruding eyes. It is huge by now, and when covered with bright red flowers in spring, it becomes, one might say, the garden's main visual attraction.

Hokyoji Temple

A "dry landscape" garden situated to the north of the temple's main hall. With its central, tasteful arrangement of rocks suggesting a waterfall, it is a readily approachable work, embodying various skillful touches such as the use of long, narrow rocks to suggest a bridge. Its attractions are reinforced in spring when the double red camellia comes into bloom.

Myorenji Temple

While stone artifacts such as the five-storied pagoda on the hillock and the stone lantern are additions made in recent years, the river represented by a stretch of largish black pebbles, the granite bridge, and the stepping stones are made in a traditional, more expansive style. The whole has a dignity worthy of a garden in a great temple.

Shozenji Temple

A tsuboniwa that also functions as a roji, it is marked off into outer and inner areas by a low bamboo fence. The stepping stones made of untreated rock and set in a more or less straight line have a pleasant freedom from fussiness; functionally, they are easy to walk on, and spiritually they prepare the guest for the simplicity and calm of the tea ceremony.

Sanzen'in Temple

Hemmed in on two sides by a corridor and on two sides by buildings, this garden consists of a tasteful arrangement of a few rocks and miniature bamboos set in moss with low ferns growing around them, producing an excellent match with the white plaster walls on two sides. A masterly example of how to create a harmony of architecture and garden.

Chiekoin Temple

With the wall in the background reminiscent of a gold-leaf folding screen, the design of this garden is very much like that of a traditional landscape painting. The whole is a good example of how a vast world can be suggested in a tiny space. The stone prop that supports the earthen wall is an important compositional element in creating the overall atmosphere. Clear and uncomplicated, this garden has an extremely fresh, lucid feel.

Ryojuin Temple

A tsuboniwa with an unusual T-shaped plan, this is essntially a rock garden, with white sand suggesting the sea and rocks bordered by "waves" representing islands. Toward the end of spring, a special touch of freshness is given to this monochrome world by the white flowers of the rhododendron.

Genkoan Temple

An inner garden situated between the Kuri and the Shoin and composed of a central, hexagonal stone lantern, a single rock, and shrubbery of varying heights. The simple, casual-seeming arrangement creates in practice an effect of quality.

◄ Jurinji Temple

This garden lies between three of the temple buildings—the main hall, the Shoin, and the tea room. Near the center stands a cherry tree, 150 years old, that is known as the "Ariwara cherry" since its planting was inspired by a poem about the cherry blossom by Ariwara no Narihira, the celebrated Heian-period poet, who lived in the temple. With its design of scattered rocks of various sizes, the garden is sometimes said to represent a distant Buddhist paradise in the sea.

Murin'an

A work by the well-known garden designer Jihee Ogawa (1860–1933). An approximately 19-square-meter space surrounded on all sides by open corridors and rooms situated behind sliding screens, it serves the double purpose of bringing in light and fresh air and providing a pleasing view. The design consists of a bed of moss with two picturesque rocks and some twenty small bamboos—a simple arrangement which guarantees, conversely, that one does not tire of it. This type of appeal, which it shares with the courtyard gardens of the Kyoto Imperial Palace, represents the tsuboniwa in its earliest form.

Townhouses

*Functionally speaking, the tsuboniwa incorporated
within the characteristic townsman's house of Kyoto
served the twin function of ventilation and
illumination, but in time it came also to play
an aesthetic role as an oasis bringing intimations of
the beauty and vastness of the natural world into
the very heart of the dwelling.*

Ban Residence

A "flat" garden without a hillock but plentiful greenery. The scene is enhanced by two stone wash basins placed near the veranda and two stone lanterns. Any over-busyness that this might create is offset by the restfulness of shrubs such as camellia and sasanqua.

Ban Residence

In the center of an overall surface of black and white gravel, a rather massive stone base is surmounted by a pleasingly shaped iron lantern. A sensitive touch is provided by ten to fifteen clumps of bamboo with low-lying fern and sacred lilies growing around the base, which give a stylish feel to the garden as a whole.

Ban Residence

Another garden seen from a window of a detached guest room. The low-set, un-pretentious water basin of Kurama stone combines with the flourishing greenery to create a relaxed, leisurely mood.

Torii Residence

A low-set water basin in the shape of an old Japanese coin is placed in the center, with an an Oribe stone lantern next to it, the round and square shapes forming an interesting contrast. The garden as a whole has an air of elegant distinction that is quietly reinforced by the green of the moss.

Ueno Residence

On the eve of the celebrated Gion Festival held in Kyoto in July, it has long been the custom for certain of the old merchant families living in homes bordering the route to put their treasured folding screen paintings on show in their front rooms, which are normally used as places of business. These displays delight the eyes of the crowds strolling the streets to view the festival floats standing there in readiness for the next day. The occasional glimpse of a small private garden lying beyond the front room is a refreshing touch on a hot summer night.

Kubo Residence (Hyoki)

This garden was created by Keinen Imao, an artist and the former householder. The centerpiece is a water basin making use of a carved stone base on which a pillar once rested, possibly dating from the Kamakaura period. A square stone lantern and a *kutsunugi* stone (for use by guests as they remove their footwear) are set nearby. The sun's rays, filtered through the leaves of the trees, are an added element in the composition.

Okamura Residence

In this broad but shallow garden the chief attraction is the plants, and the feeling is correspondingly mild, with a moss-grown, picturesquely rustic wash basin and a smallish Kasuga stone lantern providing focal points. The tall fence covered with cryptomeria bark in the background evokes the austere atmosphere of a remote mountain scene, and the stretch of white pebbles suggests a stream.

Hata Residence

A typical Kyoto-style garden, with its large Kasuga lantern at the very rear and its general suggestion of the garden of a tea house. The window in the shoji permits a heart-easing view of the garden outside.

◂ Fujii Residence

A tsuboniwa situated between the rear guest room and the uncompromisingly white wall of the storehouse. A largish water basin is accompanied by a number of rocks but, unusually, there are no stepping stones as such. A small stone lantern in the center of the garden works to draw the somewhat loose arrangement more tightly together, creating a fine overall balance.

Nose Residence

The visitor's eye is straightway caught by the Kifune and Kamo rocks placed to the right and left in the entrance, providing a foretaste of the charms of the garden beyond. On the surface of the Kifune rock on the right, an attractive pattern in relief suggests the waters of a fall, calling to mind the Kifune River that is one of the sources of the Kamo River flowing through the city of Kyoto.

Nose Residence

The stone objects of this tsuboniwa, including the square lantern in the center, together with the water basin, the *kutsunugi* stone, and the stepping stones, are all made of expensive Kurama rock, while the rhapis palm and bamboo to the rear of the lantern suggest the remote Kurama mountain area near Kyoto. The garden as a whole recreates in miniature the Kitayama district, one of the scenic spots of Kyoto. ▶

Nose Residence

The main garden of the Nose Residence, which extends to a considerable depth, is hemmed in by three rooms and a corridor. Its three-dimensional appeal is created by stone objects and a variety of rocks of varying heights: a central Kasuga lantern a good two meters in height, a Sennyuji "snow-viewing" stone lantern, a wash basin, a huge Kifune rock, and so on. Each of them fits into the overall pattern, creating a garden of leisurely proportions unexpected at the rear of a townhouse.

Nose Residence

Another view of the garden from a detached guest room, which also serves as a tea room. If one splashes water on the garden with its fresh greenery, a cool breeze comes in through the bamboo blinds and fills the room. It is a splendid device for getting through muggy Kyoto summers in relative comfort.

Bokkai Residence

One passes through the gate to find the ground covered with a layer of the kind of small, black pebbles known as *nachiguro*, with flat, rectangular granite paving stones leading in a straight line to the entrance of the tea house. To the left, three stepping stones of various sizes made of Kurama rock show the way to the arbor, where guests wait for the tea ceremony to begin.

Yoshida Residence

Part of the original garden was sacrificed to make more space for rooms, but the resulting compression has in effect transformed what was a tsuboniwa of conventional design into something more taut and compelling. The hexagonal lantern, believed to be 500 to 600 years old, gives a focal point and helps provide a sense of perspective. It is a friendly garden that really comes to life in early summer when the azaleas flower.

Inoue Residence

This was designed explicitly as a roji. An original feature is the copper wash basin. There is an Oribe stone lantern, and further along the stepping stones a large Kasuga lantern. The vegetation—evergreens including pine and sasanqua—skillfully suggests a quiet scene in the remote hills.

Inoue Residence

The garden as seen through a bamboo blind, which stirs in the faint breeze that brings a touch of coolness into the room on a hot summer's day.

Mikami Residence

This tsuboniwa takes into account the views from three different rooms. Individual objects such as the stone wash basin and the *kutsunugi* stone all use superior material. Similar care on the part of the designer is apparent in the vegetation: low shrubs are chosen so as to keep the garden light, relaxed, and restful in feeling.

Nakakura Residence

During a recent remodeling of the residence, the garden too was refashioned, making use as far as possible of the original materials; it was also, presumably, reduced in size. The Kasuga stone lantern, the rock arrangements, and the stepping stones are all rather large, but a Kenninji fence and shrubbery are carefully used to maintain a balance in the composition as a whole.

Matsumura Residence

An exquisitely designed tsuboniwa for the entrance to the house. There is an Oribe stone lantern and a wash basin specially designed so that water wells up from the bottom. The combination of the white plaster wall over the wooden wainscot, and the garden itself, create the restful atmosphere characteristic of the Kyoto townhouse.

Matsumura Residence

In another Matsumura garden, the focal point is an octagonal stone lantern; an interesting feature is the mixture of old and new bamboo fencing in the background. The materials used in the garden—the wash basin, the "scenic" rocks, the stepping stones beneath the eaves, and even the plants—all come from the Kyoto area, and the garden itself is intended to represent the Kyoto basin.

Tatsumi Residence

The principal features are the Oribe stone lantern and the tall wash basin standing close to the veranda. The stepping stones that start from the large stone used by guests in removing their footwear lead to a Kasuga stone lantern, well over two meters in height. The design is typical of the tsuboniwa of a Kyoto townhouse.

Tatsumi Residence

Surrounded by a rustic-looking wall of cryptomeria bark, this garden has a smallish stone lantern, a wash basin in the shape of a tea container, and a small, oblong granite rock set on a carpet of fine gravel. The amount of greenery, neither too great nor too small, is just right to balance the stone objects and make the small space look larger than it really is.

◄ Tatsumi Residence

A view of the tsuboniwa looking down from a second-floor room. One can see, amidst the abundant greenery, the various kinds of rock from the Kyoto area—Kurama red rock, black rock from the Kamo River—that are used for the stepping stones. Tsuboniwa in Kyoto are characterized by the beauty of these stones. The right angle in the line of the copper-covered roof prevents the plan of the garden from becoming a dull rectangle.

Nishimura Residence

A veritable display case for the art of creating objects in stone. Among the objects set on a carpet of moss are a central hexagonal stone lantern from the Kamakura period, a low-set hand-washing basin, and a small stone shrine containing a Buddhist statue. The designer has kept the earthen wall low so as to let in more light, and purposely planted an old oak tree with a hollow trunk so as to give an air of austere age to what is in fact a new garden.

Ukai Residence

A garden designed as a whole to fulfill the function of a roji. The emphasis here is on the spiritually therapeutic effect of observing the gradually changing seasons. There is ample greenery, and plants are chosen that provide color in the months from autumn, through winter, and on into early spring—bushclover, maple, camellia, Japanese damson (*ume*), and others.

Private Residence

A principal feature of interest is the large *kutsunugi* (the stone on which guests step to remove their footwear) of Kurama stone. A number of rocks and an Oribe stone lantern are arranged on the moss, but in order to keep the atmosphere cheerful and relaxed in what is the tsuboniwa of an ordinary residence, care is taken not to give too much prominence to the rocks, and the shrubbery is kept low.

Private Residence

A garden designed to fulfil the double function of a roji giving access to the tea room, and a garden for viewing from within a room. The centerpiece, a massive hexagonal stone lantern, is set off by a plentiful variety of natural greenery—red pine, maples, *mokkoku* (*Ternstroemia japonica*), and azalea—and the vivid green of the moss covering the ground is particularly striking.

Gen'an

The wash basin consists of the base of a small pagoda made to contain esoteric mantras from the Muromachi period and is accompanied by a large boat-shaped rock and a movable iron lantern. When one views the garden from within, the boundary between garden and room seems to disappear completely, so that the garden becomes part of the room interior and the room a simple extension of the garden.

Gen'an

This garden fulfills the double function of roji and tsuboniwa. The stone wash basin in the foreground makes use of a pillar base-stone from a Kamakura-period Buddhist temple. Beside it stands an Oribe stone lantern, and the stepping stones lead the eye toward a Kasuga stone lantern standing at the rear of the garden.

Bellflowers, Gen'an

At the rear of the garden are grown all kinds of *chabana* —the kinds of flowers or plants placed in a vase in the tea room alcove. It is a relaxing spot, one where men and nature come together amidst the perfectly defined changes of Kyoto's seasons.

Hydrangeas, Gen'an

The feeling of the hydrangeas is almost as if they were growing in the wild. Nearby, a long, narrow stone leads the way to the rear of the garden, where a glimpse of a small family shrine gives an added touch of atmosphere.

Autumn Maple Leaves, Gen'an

Small, scarlet leaves and larger, yellow leaves from two different species of maple lie liberally scattered about the garden in a scene that has all the characteristic gaiety and sadness of late autumn.

Stepping Stones, Gen'an

From late autumn on into spring, when the deciduous trees and shrubs have shed their leaves, the stones of the garden, which were not so prominent in the summer, come into their own again. The individual features of the various types of rock combine with the scarlet camellia flowers that have fallen on the green moss below to give the garden the special beauty peculiar to winter.

Public Places

Passing through the tsuboniwa, the rays of the setting sun come into the guest room. Shadows of leaves play upon the tatami. Sunset in summer is a brief time of healing, nostalgia, and warmth—only Kyoto can offer all this.

Noguchi Residence (Karakuan)

The rear garden seen from a guest room in the distinguished *shoin* style originally brought from the mansion of Kobori Enshu (1579–1647), a tea master and garden designer of the early Edo Period. Everything—the footwear-removing stone, the wash basin, the stone lantern, and the stepping stones—is rather massive, but this is matched by the large area of the garden itself. Taken together with the green of the vegetation, the total effect is of a subtle, somewhat mysterious beauty.

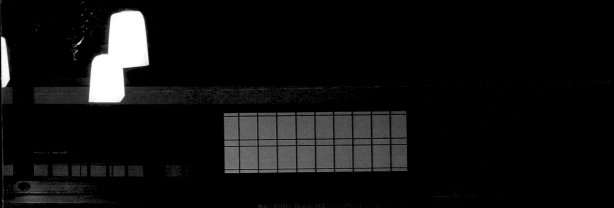

Noguchi Residence (Karakuan)

A tsuboniwa in the style of a tea house roji. A small hexagonal stone lantern is accompanied by
a low-set water basin and two rhythmically winding rows of stepping stones. Vegetation is represented by the rhapis palm that grows throughout the garden, its stems and leaves serving the
secondary function of forming a screen that effectively shields the garden from the gaze of people
in the rooms to east and west. It is astonishing how efficiently this exotic plant of the palm family,
originally from the South Pacific, suits the tsuboniwa and gives it a feeling of coolness.

Noguchi Residence (Karakuan)

This garden is new compared with the other two, but the prominence given to the wash basin, with rocks nearby and a low, square stone lantern, follows traditional practice. Seen beyond the shadowiness of the room formerly used for business, with its black-lacquered ceiling and boarded floor, the tsuboniwa impresses itself upon the senses.

Miyazaki Residence

Here, all the traditional elements of the teahouse garden are embodied in a medium-sized area of some 30 square meters. The absence of any sense of muddle is probably due to the combination with the simple beauty of the two rear walls. The vegetation, too, shows an admirable blend of taller trees such as black pine and maples with a variety of lower shrubs.

Tanaka-ya

Combining the aspects of both the roji and the tsuboniwa, this garden is distinguished by its original design—two wash basins flanking an Oribe stone lantern with a tall, hexagonal Kasuga lantern drawing the whole composition together. The moss covering the ground grows higher than the stepping stones, and the many different types of plant are kept pruned low.

Rakusho

When a wing for use as a restaurant was added to this residence, the garden was reduced in size, but it can still be viewed at close quarters from any part of the restaurant. The water from the stream on the hillock tumbles down into a pond in which giant *nishiki-goi*—the owner's pride—swim in lordly fashion. The water tumbling from the fall provides not just a pleasant sound, but a source of oxygen for the fish.

Shoeido

A tsuboniwa made on top of a modern building. The outer roji, separated off by a bamboo fence and gate, is a concise arrangement of miniature bamboo and "dragon whiskers" grass, and the inner roji likewise confines itself to the minimum elements constituting a tea garden. The visitor reaches the tea house amid the restful atmosphere created by an overall layer of black pebbles. ▶

Nakazato

A bamboo Koetsu fence separates the inner roji from the outer. The designer has kept the fence low so as to soften the picture as a whole. The stone lantern, too, is correspondingly low, and the trunks and branch formations of the shrubs are unassertive, combining with the sparse grass and moss to summon up a world of rustic simplicity.

Nakazato

This small garden is surrounded on three sides by corridors. The design is extremely simple: an Oribe stone lantern is set in gravel with seven clumps of a large species of bamboo. Added interest is provided by a fence of bamboo and wood on the west side. The result is a spare, uncloying beauty.

Tawara-ya

The rooms in this renowned inn all have their own little garden, which gives them the feeling of independent annexes. They all have ingeniously differentiated atmospheres. This particular garden is composed rather like an inner roji. Marked off by a bamboo hedge, it is full of the fresh green of flourishing shrubs and grasses.

Tawara-ya

The guest who comes into the main entrance and passes along the corridor to his room invariably glances at this tsuboniwa. A light burns in the stone lantern, and water spills from a well, both visual delights. The touch of green afforded by the rhapis palm and the flower placed over the well extend a warm welcome to each guest.

Tawara-ya

In a small space enclosed by a connecting corridor, an iron lantern originally meant for hanging is set on what was once a pillar base-stone from a Buddhist temple, resting on a surface of fine gravel. While lighting the way for the hotel guest walking along the corridor in the late afternoon or evening, the arrangement also creates a small, intimate world of its own.

Kinmata

Coming in from the front entrance and passing along a dimly lit corridor, guests of the inn encounter a tsuboniwa with white gravel and a Koetsu fence. The basin and Oribe stone lantern are in the style of a roji, but here they are for appreciation rather than practical use. The vegetation is simple, the total effect restful.

Kinmata

A tsuboniwa in the style of a roji. The fronds of the double bamboo fence are intended to suggest rain, while the stepping stones mix rocks from the Kurama and Kamo rivers, suggesting the northern outskirts of Kyoto. The hexagonal stone lantern, large but with an unpretentious, rather neglected air—the central feature —suggests a relaxing, restful stay for the visitor.

Tsuruya Yoshinobu

A garden, made on top of a modern building, which serves in part as the roji of a tea room. The central feature is a large, extremely artistic piece of Sajigawa rock (the rock is, incidentally, designated a natural national asset) from Tottori prefecture. The wash basin is made of naturally occurring granite.

Hashimoto Teru Orimono

As is shown by the pagoda, the "island" floating on a sea of white gravel symbolizes
Mt. Sumeru, said in Buddhism to stand at the center of the universe. The gentle
curves of eight types of trees are intended to suggest mountain ranges. Access to the
island is provided by the stepping stones in the sea. A stone wash basin stands on
the "beach."

Shosuikaku, Nishijin Asagi

A small, roji-style garden, bounded by a corridor, lies between a main room and a converted storehouse, which was remodeled as a display room for Nishijin fabrics. The wash basin, of superior Kurama stone, is skillfully situated in a hollow, and the trees and bushes about it are small, with gentle lines. The garden is mainly intended for viewing from within, but it is also attractive as seen from the corridor on the way to the display room.

Orinasu Museum

The group of stones suggesting a waterfall—a bold arrangement of large pieces quarried at Kifune, in the northern outskirts of Kyoto—calls to mind, to stunning effect, the swift-flowing stream that carves its way through the rock in that area. Two stone wash basins recall one to the everyday world in a fascinating blending of the concerns of nature and man.

Yamanaka Oil

The area in which this garden is situated, though within the city of Kyoto, is noted for its abundance of naturally rising spring water. The bridge over the garden's pond is of the type known as *yatsuhashi*, a form with traditionally rustic associations that has appeared in art and literature ever since the Heian period. A waterwheel, spilling water into the pond with its leisurely swimming carp, further adds to the feeling of a country scene.

Gekkeikan

The suggestion is of an island—thickly covered here with the ground plant known as "dragon whiskers" —floating on a sea of white gravel. A snow-viewing stone lantern and a few carefully placed rocks are accompanied by maple, sasanqua, and other shrubs. In late autumn, the red leaves of the maple, falling on the "shore," lament the passing of the year.

Wada Residence

Gravel, a few stepping stones, and, plumped massively in front of the storehouse, a well formed of four large stone slabs and brimming with water. Along with the practical function of protecting the storehouse from fire—so important for a merchant family—the well with its sense of style and dignity is an integral part of the composition.

Machiya Photo Museum

A small garden lurking inconspicuously at the rear of a narrow-fronted, latticed townhouse that was apparently already in existence at the beginning of the Meiji era, this is a classic specimen of the roji-type tsuboniwa, composed as it is of elements such as a stone lantern, a wash basin, and stepping stones. The startlingly large stone lantern of the Zendoji type is an extremely bold stroke that gives the garden much of its character.

Kahitsukan, Kyoto Museum of Contemporary Art

An extremely simple garden, created inside a modern building and consisting of a stretch of green moss with two rocks and a single maple tree. A large round aperture in the ceiling not only lets in light and fresh air but is an invitation to rain and snow also. The tight relationship between rooms and garden creates an integrated, distinguished world of its own.

Kasuien, Westin Miyako Kyoto

The inner garden of a building known as Kasuien, designed by the well-known Showa-era architect Togo Murano. Surrounded by lobby and corridor, it is made to be viewed from any angle. The basic design is intended to suggest the comfortable service provided by the hotel. Against a background of white gravel are set two areas of lawn in the shape of a gourd (traditionally for holding sake) and a sake cup. The feeling is utterly modern, the harmony between building and garden impressive.

Kasuien, Westin Miyako Kyoto

The design of the Kasuien profits from its location on a ridge in the hilly site of the hotel. Seen as a whole from the highest part of the building, the straight lines of the architecture and the curves of the "gourd" and "sake cup" form an attractive contrast.

Creating a Tsuboniwa—The Gen'an Garden

Choosing a Theme

The first stage in designing a garden is to decide on a theme. For instance, if the garden is intended for a shrine, one incorporates something, such as an *iwasaka* (craggy rocks at the peak of a mountain, believed to be the dwelling of the gods), associated with popular belief. If the building is in the ancient, aristocratic *shinden-zukuri* style, one creates an elegant effect by planting a pair of *ume* (Japanese damson) trees, one with white blossom, one with red, in the manner of the flat gardens enclosed by buildings and open corridors to be seen in the celebrated *Tale of Genji* picture scroll. For a Buddhist temple, the best style would probably be a "dry landscape" (*kare sansui*) garden, a uniform stretch of white sand with an arrangement of rocks that, with its rich spiritual implications, creates a suitably religious atmosphere. For a private dwelling whose owner is an adept of the tea ceremony and has his own tea room, one would make a garden in the style of a *roji*, the small garden flank-ing a pathway of stepping stones that gives immediate access to the tea room itself. For a high-class Japanese restaurant or inn where guests are served meals, one might have a bed of white sand or pebbles with, set against it like a sandbank emerging from a stretch of water, a dark green area of moss in the shape of a sake cup or gourd sake bottle. Theme and style are at once separate and inextricably tied to each other; once the former is decided on, the general technical approach to the design becomes clearer. In what follows, as a way of illustrating this point, I have based my discussion on a garden (see pages 76-77) that I designed in 1997 for an establishment called Gen'an, which is located in the Nishijin area, the traditional textile center.

From the Edo period (1603–1867) on into the Showa era (1926–1989), the vicinity was dominated by the premises of dealers in raw silk, and was so prosperous that it was popularly known as the Senryo-ga-tsuji ("The Million Dollar District"). Gen'an is a typical Kyoto *machiya* merchant-class townhouse—of the type known as an "eel's lair," with

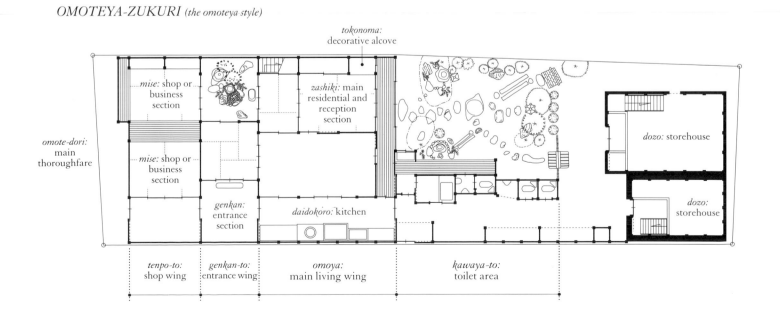

OMOTEYA-ZUKURI *(the omoteya style)*

tokonoma: decorative alcove

mise: shop or business section

zashiki: main residential and reception section

omote-dori: main thoroughfare

mise: shop or business section

dozo: storehouse

genkan: entrance section

daidokoro: kitchen

dozo: storehouse

tenpo-to: shop wing

genkan-to: entrance wing

omoya: main living wing

kawaya-to: toilet area

a facade about 10 meters in width and a depth of about 30 meters. The particular architectural style, known as *omoteya-zukuri*, persisted from the early Edo period (sevententh century) right up to the Taisho era (1912–1926). It has three main wings, all constructed separately: a wing for displaying wares or conducting business (*mise*), a main—residential and reception—wing (*omoya*), and at the rear a storehouse for keeping the raw silk in which the family dealt, so that it did not dry out (see illustration on page 113). This mode of construction was very costly; by further linking the various sections with an entrance wing (*genkan*) and an area housing toilets, two spaces were formed in which tsuboniwa could be constructed.

The main objective of my project was to restore the tsuboniwa—which had been dismantled—in the open space facing the *genkan* wing that links the *mise* and the main structure. The first purpose of this garden, as is appropriate to the entrance of a merchant home, must be to present an attractive face to potential customers. The style of the *zashiki* suggested the taste typical of a devotee of the tea ceremony, so I felt that the type of garden centering on the *tsukubai*—the low-set water basin at which participants in the ceremony rinse their hands—might be appropriate. Futhermore, the design should take into account three considerations, corresponding to the three angles from which the garden would be viewed: first, as already mentioned, the effect on potential customers coming into the entrance; next, the need of family members living in the *zashiki* section for good ventilation and fresh air; and thirdly the view from the shop and business section. At the rear of its *zashiki* section, the residence in question has a tsuboniwa (see pages 78, 79) of unusual size and sophisticated design for a townhouse, suggesting that the resident at the time was a man of considerable taste and refinement. The two gardens, being separated by the main residential section, can be viewed independently, but I felt that they should have some kind of organic link (see figure 1), and that the restoration of the garden in the *genkan* entrance would give new life to the whole *machiya* as a pleasant place to live in.

Designing the Garden

In cases where the house is divided from that next door by a plaster wall, it is usually assumed that, in a tsuboniwa in the *roji* style, one will create a rustic effect by using a fence such as a Kenninji (split-bamboo) or rush fence, or by facing the wall behind the garden with cryptomeria bark. However, I wanted to create a new effect by taking the fullest advantage of things as they stood. Since commissioning the creation of a garden is, ultimately, one of the higher forms of self-indulgence, the owner naturally wants his small garden to feel as spacious as possible, and one must respect his wishes. Thus I racked my brains to think of some way of expanding the total picture by bringing in the mortar wall at the rear. The idea I came up with was to use the light falling through the space open to the sky in order to throw a triangular image suggesting Mt. Fuji onto the wall. The eaves of the secondary roof of the main structure and those newly added to the *mise* were thus used to cast two clear-cut diagonal lines onto the wall (see figure 2).

fig. 1

fig. 2

fig. 3 View from the zashiki.

fig. 4 View from the shop.

fig. 5 View from the entrance.

Next, though, I came up against a major problem involving the structure of the building itself: I realized that instead of the bare earth needed to provide the soil essential to the garden, I must create it on an already existing concrete floor. In the end, I resigned myself to doing without soil in the design. A dozen or so rocks left lying in a corner of the rear garden gave some idea of the design of the original. An extremely well-shaped, Mt. Fuji–style basin made of natural pinkish Kurama rock, and a dismembered Oribe-style stone lantern, had also survived. I was torn between a desire to recycle these and a desire to do something completely new. But then it occurred to me that a single garden had no need of two Mt. Fujis, and I gave up the idea of using the old *tsukubai*. I also gave up the Oribe stone lantern, since this would have required making a hole in the concrete floor to receive its base, which would have been impossible. I was still debating what to do when I came across a basin made of the Shirakawa stone found in the Mt. Daimonji area of Sakyo ward, Kyoto city; it had an enormously attractive texture with a hint of pink in it, and had originally formed the base of a *hokyoin-to* (a type of short stone pagoda) made in the early Muromachi period. The hole for the water was too large to be ideal, but the pleasantly weathered relief carving on the upturned-lotus pedestal was what decided me.

The garden measures only 3 meters by 3.5 meters, so I chose a small washbasin (*tsukubai*), and kept the number of stones with definite functions down to the smallest number possible without detriment to those functions. So for the "hot water stone" (on which water for use in the tea ceremony is placed) and "lamp stand stone" (on which a lamp is placed for use in a tea ceremony held at night) I chose rocks that were flat top and bottom, and, for the *kutsunugi-ishi* (on which guests step when removing their footwear) and *mae-ishi* ("forestone," placed before the basin containing the water in which the guests rinse their hands), rocks that were a good shape, small yet providing the minimum necessary space to step on. I gave up the idea of stepping stones, however, because of the size of the garden, and, by way of *keiseki* (an im-

portant rock that is effective artistically without fulfilling any other specific function), made use of a boat-shaped, two-stepped stone that I found behind the family storehouse. I decided that in view of the need to make the garden interesting as viewed from three different angles, it was important to select stones with varied, irregularly shaped faces. For the floor, in the absence of earth, medium-sized Jodoji-ishi pebbles seemed most suitable.

Where plants were concerned, I decided on rhapis palm, which would give an added touch of coolness in a Kyoto townhouse designed chiefly with the heat of summer in mind. A stone lantern was needed too, but since the base could not be buried in the concrete floor, it must be kept short for the sake of stability, and I decided that the type that simply rested on a heavy, stable pedestal might be best. In the rear garden, I discovered the base stone from a Kasuga-type lantern, a large, very solid-looking piece of blackish Shirakawa rock, which I thought might do as the pedestal if I placed an iron lantern of the movable type on top of it. I told myself fancifully that the stone would surely be pleased to find itself used properly as the pedestal of a lantern, the role for which it had originally been intended, rather than lying around as a cast-out.

The all-important iron lantern itself, though, was the problem. I went around the antique shops, but could find nothing suitable. So I decided to make do with a new piece, and went to have a look at the catalogues in a shop dealing in ironwork; but the latest models all lacked character. Then I came across a battered catalogue of samples, at least ten years old, lying inconspicuously in a corner of the shop. In the section showing lanterns of the type that stands on a pedestal without having its base buried in the soil, I found listed a piece "in the Yojiro style" (Tsuji Yojiro was a Muromachi-period artist in cast metal). The proprietor of the shop told me that it was no longer being made, so I got him to inquire of the manufacturers, who came up with just one, which had been lying half-forgotten in their storehouse. He ordered it for me, and I found it to be rather ancient and weathered-looking, which suited my purpose admirably; the price, moreover, was what it had been when it was first made—all in all, a real find. I drew sketches of the garden as I wanted it to look from the three important angles (see figures 3, 4, and 5), added a rough plan, and embarked on discussions with the specialist artisans who were to put it together.

The Garden in the Making

I made arrangements with the artisans to obtain the necessary rocks and stones, then we decided on the general layout and had the materials brought in (see figure 6). Remembering that the garden would be viewed from three sides, I placed the central feature, the waterbasin, not in the most stable position, i.e., in the center as seen from the *gen-*

fig. 6

kan, but a little toward the room. The stone lantern went to a spot neither too near nor too far away, thus concentrating the principal features in the center of the garden and preventing a scattered effect. Even so, to avoid creating a crowded feeling, I placed the boat-shaped rock, chosen for its artistic shape, some distance away, closer to the wall; the result was to suggest a boat crossing the "sea" of white gravel. I placed the rocks swiftly, without too much hesitation, adjusting from moment to moment as the need struck

me; to do it in this way gives a sense of dynamism to the resulting garden.

The following day we did the arranging of the plants (see figure 7). We set the rhapis palm in a shallow flower pot, hiding the pot by making a mound of earth to cover it. With a protective covering of moss to prevent the earth from being washed away by rain, the mound, though not high, succeeded in suggesting the atmosphere of the hillock that is a feature of larger gardens. A short nandin plant was set by the boat, and ferns were placed at several points around the base of the rocks. In both cases, I used rounded tiles from the eaves of old temples instead of pots. After moss had been planted to grow on the pedestal of the iron lantern, nothing remained but to place the latter on its pedestal, and the garden would be complete.

With time, a garden grows and settles in. Figure 1 shows the tsuboniwa two years after it was first made, seen through the open shoji of the *mise* section. Although the rhapis has not much soil, it has grown steadily, and its leaves rustle in the slightest breeze. At some point or other, a small variety of begonia has seeded itself in the space between the water basin and the "lamp stand" stone. A pleasant if unexpected intruder, it makes me wonder afresh at the hardiness of nature that set it to grow here on stones with no soil. Since it gets no direct sunlight, it has only a very few flowers, but the assymmetrical arrangement of large and small leaves has individuality, and it will serve each year as a pleasing harbinger of early autumn. My tsuboniwa has grown into a spot where one can truly enjoy the feeling of being "in the town yet amidst nature."

fig. 7

Types of Stone Lantern

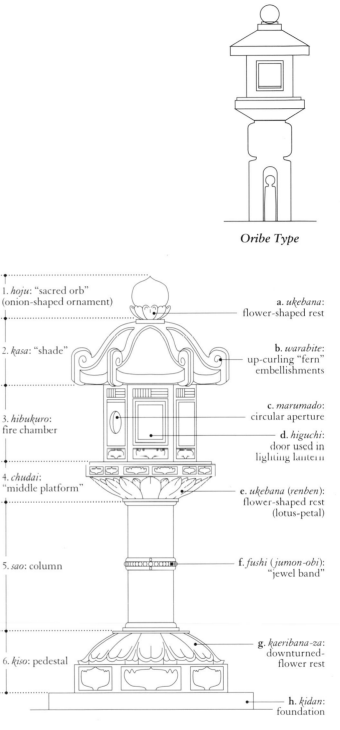

Oribe Type

In his "tea gardens" (*roji*, the pathway-cum-garden giving access to a tea room), the celebrated late-sixteenth century tea master Sen no Rikyu is said to have been the first to utilize for lighting and decorative purposes selected specimens of stone lanterns (*ishi-doro*) obtained from shrines or temples, where they had originally been intended to provide light for the deities enshrined there. Subsequently, another tea master, Furuta Oribe, felt the need for a type of lantern more specifically suited to the tea garden—not tall and standing on a pedestal, but shorter, with its supporting column partly buried in the ground, and thus capable of illuminating a low-lying washbasin or the garden path. Since the number of fine specimens available from shrines and temples was limited, large numbers of imitations were made, and the lanterns that had provided the original models came to be known as *honka*.

Names of types of stone lanterns fall, by and large, into three categories: 1) those taken from the names of the temples or shrines possessing the *honka* or other especially fine examples; 2) those describing the design or other visible feature of the lantern; 3) those taking the name of the designer or some master of the tea ceremony who particularly favored the design. Examples include, respectively, 1) Kasuga type, Nishinoya type, Zendoji type; 2) hexagonal type, octagonal type, *mizubotaru* type; 3) Oribe-type. Some names are combinations of types 1 and 2, as in the case of Sennyuji-*yukimi* lanterns, where the name of a temple is joined to *yukimi* ("snow-viewing," because the broad "shade" (*kasa*) of the lantern provides an ideal surface for snow to settle on in a picturesque fashion).

1. *hoju*: "sacred orb" (onion-shaped ornament)

2. *kasa*: "shade"

3. *hibukuro*: fire chamber

4. *chudai*: "middle platform"

5. *sao*: column

6. *kiso*: pedestal

a. *ukebana*: flower-shaped rest

b. *warabite*: up-curling "fern" embellishments

c. *marumado*: circular aperture

d. *higuchi*: door used in lighting lantern

e. *ukebana* (*renben*): flower-shaped rest (lotus-petal)

f. *fushi* (*jumon-obi*): "jewel band"

g. *kaeribana-za*: downturned-flower rest

h. *kidan*: foundation

The Kasuga-type Stone Lantern

The Oribe-type Stone Lantern

The name derives from the fact that Furuta Oribe, the celebrated master of the tea ceremony, is said to have favored this type of stone lantern. Possibly the finest type of originally designed lantern, it is ideally suited to the small space afforded by the tsuboniwa. There is no *honka*, but the earliest known specimen dates from 1615. Many such lanterns have a relief carving of a standing figure on the lower part of the supporting pillar; some scholars see this as a figure of the Virgin Mary.

The Kasuga-type Stone Lantern

The most popular form of stone lantern; the name is applied in general to lanterns with a hexagonal form and composed of six elements (see diagram).

The Nishinoya-type Stone Lantern

The name derives from the fact that the original stood before the Nishinoya, one of the structures of the Kasuga Shrine in Nara. The simple, clear-cut beauty created by the fact that all its basic components are square has made it popular among devotees of the tea ceremony, who often use it in their *roji*.

The Mizubotaru-type Stone Lantern

The *honka* of this type stands by the lake in front of the En-rindo, a part of the Katsura Imperial Villa. The name, which means "firefly over the water," is said to allude to a poem written by Prince Yakahito, seventh head of one of the main branches of the imperial family, in which he relates how he mistook the reflection of the light of a lantern on the other side of a pond for a firefly flying above the water.

The Sennyuji "Snow-viewing" Stone Lantern

The four legs, each of which is rhomboid in section, are spread rather more widely than in the Katsura lantern, and the shade is surmounted by a *hoju* ("sacred orb," a vaguely onion-shaped ornament). The fire chamber and the *chudai* ("middle platform") on which it rests are both octagonal. As a whole the shape, attractively free from anything excessive or intrusive, is eminently suited to provide a decorative feature in a garden. The original is in the garden in front of the Imperial Chamber of the Sennyuji temple.

The Kodaiji-type Stone Lantern

The shade (*kasa*) bears, in relief, chrysanthemum and paulownia crests, both of which were used by Toyotomi Hideyoshi, who had associations with the Kodaiji temple after which this type of lantern is named.

The Zendoji-type Stone Lantern

The original (*honka*) is in the Zendoji temple. Created especially for use in a garden, this type is characterized by its rather squat appearance. The articles used in the tea ceremony depicted in relief on the fire chamber indicate that it was favored by adepts of the ceremony. Note that the fire chamber of the lantern in the Machiya Photo Museum (page 107) deviates from the standard.

The "Signpost"-type Stone Lantern

An imitation of the stone signposts used on highways in pre-modern times, with a fire-chamber carved into it so that it can be used as a lantern. There is no fixed design.

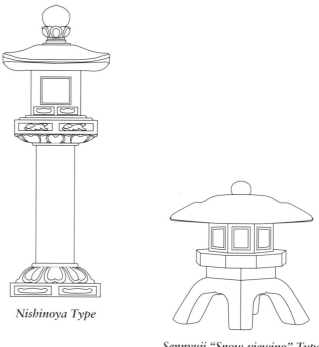

Nishinoya Type

Sennyuji "Snow-viewing" Type

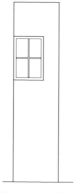

"Signpost" Type

INDEX

Ariwara no Narihira 43

Ban Residence 46, 48, 49
Bochuseki 13
Bokkai Residence 60
Buddhism vii

chabana 79
Chiekoin temple 39
Chosetsu vii
chudai 118

Daisen'in temple viii, 18, 31
Dongein temple 34
dry landscape viii, xi, 17, 18, 22, 35, 113

Edo period vii, ix, x, 114
eel's lair viii, 113
Enrindo 118

Fujii Residence 55
Fujitsubo, Kyoto Imperial Palace vii, 3
Furuta Oribe 117

Gekkeikan 105
Gen'an 76, 78, 79, 113–16
Genkoan temple 41
Gion festival viii, 51
Great Tenmei Fire x

Hagitsubo, Kyoto Imperial Palace vii, 4
hanare-zashiki ix, xi
Hashimoto Teru Orimono 100
Hata Residence 55
Heian period vii, 4
Higyosha 3
hoju 118
Hokongoin temple 21
hokyoin-to 115
Hokyoji temple 35
Honen'in temple 32
honka 117

imperial palace vii, viii, 43
Inoue Residence 62, 63
ishi-doro 117
Ishi-tsubo viii
Itoya Hatcho ix
Itoya-machi ix
iwasaka 113

Jodoji-ishi 115
Jurinji temple 43

Kahitsukan, Kyoto Museum of Contemporary
   Art 108
Kamakura period vii, viii
Kamigamo Shrine 6
Kamigyo ix
Kamo River 56
Kamo rocks 56, 71, 97
Kanchiin 22
Kanmin garden, Zuihoin temple 19
kare-sansui viii, xi, 113
Kasuga stone lantern 14, 53, 55, 58, 62, 65, 69, 78,
   87, 115, 117, 118
Kasuien, Westin Miyako Kyoto 110, 112
Katsura Imperial Villa 118
Keinen Imao 52
keiseki 115
Kenninji fence 65, 114
Kifune River 56
Kifune rock 56, 58, 102
Kinmata 96, 97
Kinmon Incident x
Kiritsubo vii
Kitayama 23, 56
Kobori Enshu 82
Kodaiji temple 28, 118
Kodaiji-type stone lantern 118
Koetsu fence 90, 96
Koshoji temple 15
Kubo Residence (Hyoki) 52
Kurama mountain area 56
Kurama stone 49, 60, 71, 74, 97, 101, 115
kutsunugi-ishi x, 52, 56, 64, 74, 115
Kyokusui Garden, Matsunoo Shrine 8, 9
Kyoo Gokokuji 22
Kyoto vii, viii, ix, x, xi

machiya vii, x, xi, 113, 114
Machiya Photo Museum 107, 118
mae-ishi 115
Matsumura Residence 66, 67
Matsunoshita-ya, Fushimi Inari Shrine 7
Meiji era x
meisho viii
merchant class viii, x
Mikami Residence 64
Minamoto no Yoritomo viii
mise 114
Mitarashi River 8

Miyazaki Residence 86
Mizubotaru-type stone lantern 117, 118
mokkoku 75
Momoyama period vii, x
Mt. Daimonji 115
Mt. Fuji 114, 115
Mt. Sumeru 100
Murin'an 43
Muromachi period viii
Myorenji temple 36

nachiguro 60
Nakakura Residence 65
Nakazato 90, 91
Nanyoin temple 14
Nara period vii
Ninnaji temple 10
Nishijin 113
nishiki-goi 88
Nishimura Residence 72
Nishinoya-type stone lantern 117, 118
Nishijin Fire ix
niwa vii
Noguchi Residence (Karakuan) 82, 84, 85
Nose Residence 56, 58, 59

Ogawa Jihee 43
Okamura Residence 53
omoteya ix, x
omoteya-zukuri viii, 114
omoya viii, ix, 114
Onin war viii
Oribe-style stone lantern 50, 62, 66, 69, 74, 78, 87,
   91, 96, 115, 117
Orinasu Museum 102
Osuzumi-dokoro vii
Otomo Sorin 19

Pillow Book vii

Rakusho 88
Reikanji temple 30
Reiun'in viii
roji x, xi, 20, 62, 75, 78, 87, 93, 96, 97, 101, 107, 113,
   114, 117, 118
Rokudo Garden, Nanzenji temple 12, 13
Ryojuin temple 40
Ryusentei vii

Saiho Nunnery 20
Sajigawa rock 98

samurai residence   viii
Sanzen'in temple   38
Sei Shonagon   vii
Seiryoden   vii, 4
Sen no Rikyu   x, 20, 117
Sennyuji "snow-viewing" stone lantern   58, 117, 118
Sennyuji temple   118
Senryo-ga-tsuji   113
shinden   vii
shinden-zukuri   vii, 4, 113
Shirakawa stone   115
Shoeido   88
shoin-zukuri   viii, 82
Shojokein temple   25
Shosuikaku, Nishijin Asagi   101
Shozenji temple   37
"Signpost"-type stone lantern   118
Sorenji temple   23
stepping stones   x
stone lanterns   117
storehouses   ix

Taikenmon'in   21
Taikoan temple   29
Taira no Kiyomori   viii
Taisho era   x, 114
Tale of Genji   vii
Tanaka-ya   87
Tatsumi Residence   69, 71
Tawara-ya   93, 94, 95
tea garden   7
Teishi   vii
temples   vii
Togo Murano   110
Tokaian temple   17
Tokugawa shogunate   x
Torii Residence   50
Torin'in temple   17
Totekiko Garden, Ryogen'in temple   26
townhouse   vii, viii, x
Toyotomi Hideyoshi   viii, 118
tsubo   vii
tsuboniwa   vii
Tsuji Yojiro   115

tsukubai   x, 114, 115
Tsurezure-gusa   vii
Tsuruya Yoshinobu   98

Ueno Residence   51, 73

Wada Residence   106

Yakahito   118
Yamanaka Oil   103
yatsuhashi   103
Yojiro style   115
Yomogi no Tsubo   viii
Yoshida Kenko   vii
Yoshida Residence   61

zashiki   xi, 114
Zen   vii, viii, 17
Zendoji temple   118
Zendoji-type stone lantern   107, 117, 118
Zuishin'in temple   11

坪庭
Landscapes for Small Spaces

2002 年 6 月 28 日　第 1 刷発行
2003 年 4 月 15 日　第 3 刷発行

著　者　水野克比古
発行者　畑野文夫
発行所　講談社インターナショナル株式会社
　　　　〒112-8652 東京都文京区音羽 1-17-14
　　　　電話　03-3944-6493（編集部）
　　　　　　　03-3944-6492（営業部・業務部）
　　　　ホームページ　http://www.kodansha-intl.co.jp

印刷所　株式会社サンエムカラー
製本所　株式会社サンエムカラー

落丁本・乱丁本は購入書店名を明記のうえ、小社業務部宛にお送りください。送料小社負担にてお取替えします。なお、この本についてのお問い合わせは、編集部宛にお願いいたします。本書の無断複写（コピー）、転載は著作権法の例外を除き、禁じられています。

定価はカバーに表示してあります。

Copyright © 2002 by Katsuhiko Mizuno
Printed in Japan
ISBN 4-7700-2874-1